THIS JOURNAL BELONGS TO:

# ONE
## *Question*
# A DAY

# MY LIFE

## *So Far*

**A DAILY JOURNAL FOR RECORDING
YOUR LIFE STORY**

Castle Point Books
*New York*

One Question a Day: My Life So Far.

Copyright © 2018 by St. Martin's Press.

All rights reserved. Printed in China.

For information, address St. Martin's Press, 175 Fifth Avenue, New York, N.Y. 10010.

www.stmartins.com

The Castle Point Books trademark is owned by Castle Point Publications, LLC.
Castle Point books are published and distributed by St. Martin's Press.

ISBN 978-1-250-30410-0
ISBN 978-1-250-20277-2

Our books may be purchased in bulk for promotional, educational, or business use. Please
contact your local bookseller or the Macmillan Corporate and Premium Sales
Department at 1-800-221-7945, extension 5442, or by e-mail at
MacmillanSpecialMarkets@macmillan.com.

First Edition: October 2018

10 9 8 7 6 5 4 3 2 1

## How to use this journal:

Enjoy writing the story of your life, one question at a time, with *One Question a Day: My Life So Far.* From the day that you were born, to the lessons you learned in adolescence, to the events that shifted your worldview, it's time to tell the tale of how you became the person you are today. Let each daily question (or set of questions) stir your thoughts, steer your pen, and guide you effortlessly through the journaling process.

Keep this book in easy reach and have fun building your autobiography one page at a time.

We all have a story to tell.
Let's hear yours!

*1*

What is your birthdate?
Describe what you know about
the day you were born.

_____

_____

_____

_____

_____

_____

_____

_____

_____

_____

_____

_____

_____

_____

2

What is your hometown and what
influence did it have on you?

_____

_____

_____

_____

_____

_____

_____

_____

_____

_____

_____

_____

# 3

What was going on in the world around
the time that you were born?

_____

_____

_____

_____

_____

_____

_____

_____

_____

_____

_____

_____

4

Describe your appearance as a baby.
Whom did you most resemble?

_____

_____

_____

_____

_____

_____

_____

_____

_____

_____

_____

_____

## 5

Who was present at your birth?
Who visited you soon after you were born?

_____

_____

_____

_____

_____

_____

_____

_____

_____

_____

_____

_____

6

Were you a healthy baby?
Describe any struggles you had.

_____

_____

_____

_____

_____

_____

_____

_____

_____

_____

_____

_____

_____

# 7

What are your parents' full names?
Where did they grow up?

_____

_____

_____

_____

_____

_____

_____

_____

_____

_____

_____

_____

_____

_____

*8*

Describe your mother as a parent.

_____

_____

_____

_____

_____

_____

_____

_____

_____

_____

_____

_____

9

Describe your father as a parent.

_____

_____

_____

_____

_____

_____

_____

_____

_____

_____

_____

10

How and why did your parents choose
your first and middle names?

_____

_____

_____

_____

_____

_____

_____

_____

_____

_____

_____

//

What was your first word? First food?
What other firsts do you know about?

_____

_____

_____

_____

_____

_____

_____

_____

_____

_____

_____

_____

# 12

How well did you sleep as a baby?
How does this compare to now?

_____

_____

_____

_____

_____

_____

_____

_____

_____

_____

_____

_____

_____

# 13

How active were you as a child?
When did you start to crawl and walk?

_____

_____

_____

_____

_____

_____

_____

_____

_____

_____

_____

*14*

Describe your first home.
How long did you live there?

_____

_____

_____

_____

_____

_____

_____

_____

_____

_____

_____

_____

# 15

Were you an only child, or did you have siblings?
How has this defined you?

_____

_____

_____

_____

_____

_____

_____

_____

_____

_____

_____

_____

# 16

What is your earliest memory?

_____

_____

_____

_____

_____

_____

_____

_____

_____

_____

_____

_____

## 17

What traits did you have as a baby
that you still have today?

_____

_____

_____

_____

_____

_____

_____

_____

_____

_____

_____

_____

# 18

What stories have your parents
told about you as a baby?

_____
_____
_____
_____
_____
_____
_____
_____
_____
_____
_____
_____
_____
_____
_____

## 19

What relics have you (or your family)
saved from your infancy?

_____

_____

_____

_____

_____

_____

_____

_____

_____

_____

_____

_____

# 20

Do you have any photos of yourself as a baby?
Describe your favorite one.

_____

_____

_____

_____

_____

_____

_____

_____

_____

_____

_____

_____

_____

_____

# 21

What were you like as a toddler?

---

---

---

---

---

---

---

---

---

---

---

---

---

# 22

When did you lose your first tooth?
What other early childhood milestones
can you recount?

_____

_____

_____

_____

_____

_____

_____

_____

_____

_____

_____

_____

# 23

Describe a time in your childhood
when you got into trouble.

_____

_____

_____

_____

_____

_____

_____

_____

_____

_____

_____

_____

# 24

Describe your childhood bedroom.

_____

_____

_____

_____

_____

_____

_____

_____

_____

_____

_____

_____

_____

## 25

Were you a healthy child? What memories
do you have of being home sick from school?

_____

_____

_____

_____

_____

_____

_____

_____

_____

_____

_____

_____

# 26

What was the name of your primary school,
and what do you remember about it?

_____

_____

_____

_____

_____

_____

_____

_____

_____

_____

_____

_____

# 27

What do you remember
about your first day of school?

_____

_____

_____

_____

_____

_____

_____

_____

_____

_____

_____

_____

# 28

How did you handle big changes as a kid?

_____

_____

_____

_____

_____

_____

_____

_____

_____

_____

_____

_____

# 29

When did you learn how to read, and what
were your favorite kinds of books?

_____

_____

_____

_____

_____

_____

_____

_____

_____

_____

_____

# 30

What were you like in grade school?

_____

_____

_____

_____

_____

_____

_____

_____

_____

_____

_____

_____

_____

# 31

How would teachers at school have described you?

_____

_____

_____

_____

_____

_____

_____

_____

_____

_____

_____

_____

_____

# 32

What awards or recognition did you receive as a kid?

_____

_____

_____

_____

_____

_____

_____

_____

_____

_____

_____

_____

# 33

Did you ever break any bones?
If so, which ones and how?

_____

_____

_____

_____

_____

_____

_____

_____

_____

_____

_____

_____

# 34

How do your parents and siblings describe
your personality as a kid?

_____

_____

_____

_____

_____

_____

_____

_____

_____

_____

_____

_____

## 35

What made you happy when you were younger?

_____

_____

_____

_____

_____

_____

_____

_____

_____

_____

_____

_____

# 36

What is one thing you would change
about your childhood?

_____

_____

_____

_____

_____

_____

_____

_____

_____

_____

_____

_____

_____

## 37

What is your most vivid childhood memory?

_____

_____

_____

_____

_____

_____

_____

_____

_____

_____

_____

_____

# 38

Do you know the meaning of your family name?
What stories have you heard about your ancestors?

_____

_____

_____

_____

_____

_____

_____

_____

_____

_____

_____

## 39

Were your parents married?
What was your perspective on their
relationship as a kid?

_____

_____

_____

_____

_____

_____

_____

_____

_____

_____

_____

_____

_____

40

How did your parents meet?
What else do you know about their
story/relationship?

_____

_____

_____

_____

_____

_____

_____

_____

_____

_____

_____

_____

_____

# 41

Who was stricter, your mother or
your father? Give an example.

_____

_____

_____

_____

_____

_____

_____

_____

_____

_____

_____

_____

_____

# 42

What did you daydream about
when you were younger?

_____

_____

_____

_____

_____

_____

_____

_____

_____

_____

_____

_____

_____

# 43

Describe a time when you were disciplined
for something you did wrong.

_____

_____

_____

_____

_____

_____

_____

_____

_____

_____

_____

_____

_____

44

How did your family earn money,
and what did you learn from their work ethic?

_____

_____

_____

_____

_____

_____

_____

_____

_____

_____

_____

# 45

How did your family compare to others in the
neighborhood? How did this make you feel?

_____

_____

_____

_____

_____

_____

_____

_____

_____

_____

_____

_____

# 46

Were you a picky eater?

What food do you remember hating?

_____

_____

_____

_____

_____

_____

_____

_____

_____

_____

_____

_____

_____

# 47

What was your favorite food as a child,
and how do you feel about that food now?

_____

_____

_____

_____

_____

_____

_____

_____

_____

_____

_____

_____

_____

# 48

Did you have a family pet?
If so, what was it, and how did you feel about it?

_____

_____

_____

_____

_____

_____

_____

_____

_____

_____

_____

_____

_____

# 49

In what ways did your family support
you while you were growing up?

_____

_____

_____

_____

_____

_____

_____

_____

_____

_____

_____

_____

_____

_____

# 50

Describe your siblings, if you had any, and how
they were different from you in childhood.

_____

_____

_____

_____

_____

_____

_____

_____

_____

_____

_____

_____

# 51

What drove you crazy when you were little?

_____

_____

_____

_____

_____

_____

_____

_____

_____

_____

_____

# 52

What was your happiest childhood summer like?

_____

_____

_____

_____

_____

_____

_____

_____

_____

_____

_____

_____

_____

# 53

What were your favorite summer activities?

---

 

# 54

Did you learn to swim?
If so, describe how and when.

_____

_____

_____

_____

_____

_____

_____

_____

_____

_____

_____

_____

_____

## 55

What were your favorite winter activities?

_____

_____

_____

_____

_____

_____

_____

_____

_____

_____

_____

_____

_____

# 56

What did you love doing with your
friends while growing up?

---
---
---
---
---
---
---
---
---
---
---

## 57

What did you do with your friends that scared you
(or scares you now, looking back)?

_____

_____

_____

_____

_____

_____

_____

_____

_____

_____

_____

_____

# 58

Describe your most memorable birthday party.

_____

_____

_____

_____

_____

_____

_____

_____

_____

_____

_____

_____

_____

# 59

How did your family celebrate major holidays?

_____

_____

_____

_____

_____

_____

_____

_____

_____

_____

_____

60

What was your favorite holiday? Why?

_____

_____

_____

_____

_____

_____

_____

_____

_____

_____

_____

_____

# 61

Which relatives did you visit the most?

_____

_____

_____

_____

_____

_____

_____

_____

_____

_____

_____

_____

# 62

What traditions did you have year after year?
Which one stands out the most?

_____

_____

_____

_____

_____

_____

_____

_____

_____

_____

_____

_____

# 63

What was your favorite toy or game when you were small? Describe one memory of playing with it.

_____

_____

_____

_____

_____

_____

_____

_____

_____

_____

_____

_____

_____

# 64

What were your favorite candies or treats as a kid?
What memories do these treats bring back?

_____

_____

_____

_____

_____

_____

_____

_____

_____

_____

_____

_____

## 65

What did you like best about yourself as a kid?

_____

_____

_____

_____

_____

_____

_____

_____

_____

_____

_____

_____

# 66

Was there anything you wanted to change
about yourself when you were little? Did you
succeed in changing it?

_____

_____

_____

_____

_____

_____

_____

_____

_____

_____

_____

_____

_____

# 67

Did you prefer to spend most of your time
alone or in the company of others?

_____

_____

_____

_____

_____

_____

_____

_____

_____

_____

_____

_____

_____

# 68

What characters from television, film, or books
did you identify with as a child?

_____

_____

_____

_____

_____

_____

_____

_____

_____

_____

_____

69

What were your hobbies?

_____

_____

_____

_____

_____

_____

_____

_____

_____

_____

_____

_____

# 70

Who in your family was the funniest?
What was the funniest thing he/she said or did?

_____

_____

_____

_____

_____

_____

_____

_____

_____

_____

_____

_____

_____

# 71

What was the most exciting gift
you received as a child?

_____

_____

_____

_____

_____

_____

_____

_____

_____

_____

_____

_____

# 72

Who was your favorite teacher in primary
school? What was he/she like?

_____

_____

_____

_____

_____

_____

_____

_____

_____

_____

_____

_____

# 73

What fads (toys, games, jewelry, etc.) were
popular when you were growing up?

_____

_____

_____

_____

_____

_____

_____

_____

_____

_____

_____

_____

# 74

How much freedom did you have as a kid?

_____

_____

_____

_____

_____

_____

_____

_____

_____

_____

_____

_____

_____

# 75

Who were your closest childhood friends?

_____

_____

_____

_____

_____

_____

_____

_____

_____

_____

_____

# 76

What do you remember fondly about
your childhood best friend?

_____

_____

_____

_____

_____

_____

_____

_____

_____

_____

_____

_____

# 77

What are you grateful to have had (or done) as a child?

_____

_____

_____

_____

_____

_____

_____

_____

_____

_____

_____

_____

# 78

Whom did you confide in as a kid?

_____

_____

_____

_____

_____

_____

_____

_____

_____

_____

_____

_____

# 79

What made you cry as a kid?

_____

_____

_____

_____

_____

_____

_____

_____

_____

_____

_____

_____

_____

_____

# 80

Were you ever away from home for long stretches
of time as a child? Describe how you dealt with that.

_____

_____

_____

_____

_____

_____

_____

_____

_____

_____

_____

_____

_____

## 81

What was the most embarrassing
moment in your childhood?

_____

_____

_____

_____

_____

_____

_____

_____

_____

_____

_____

# 82

During your school years, how would your
friends have described you?

_____

_____

_____

_____

_____

_____

_____

_____

_____

_____

_____

_____

_____

# 83

What did you enjoy most and least about school?

_____

_____

_____

_____

_____

_____

_____

_____

_____

_____

_____

_____

# 84

How did you earn money as a kid?
What did you spend it on?

---
---
---
---
---
---
---
---
---
---
---
---

## 85

Did you have a stay-at-home parent,
or did your parents both work? How does this
influence your perspective on raising kids?

_____

_____

_____

_____

_____

_____

_____

_____

_____

_____

_____

_____

_____

# 86

Who was your first crush?
What made this person so special?

_____

_____

_____

_____

_____

_____

_____

_____

_____

_____

_____

_____

# 87

Were you popular, unpopular, or in between? Why?

_____

_____

_____

_____

_____

_____

_____

_____

_____

_____

_____

_____

# 88

Were you a risk-taker as a kid, or did you play it safe?

_____

_____

_____

_____

_____

_____

_____

_____

_____

_____

_____

_____

# 89

If you had siblings, what activities
did you enjoy with them?

_____

_____

_____

_____

_____

_____

_____

_____

_____

_____

_____

_____

_____

90

Were you close to your siblings?
If you had no siblings, did you wish for some?

_____

_____

_____

_____

_____

_____

_____

_____

_____

_____

_____

_____

# 91

What did your parents think of your closest friends?

_____

_____

_____

_____

_____

_____

_____

_____

_____

_____

_____

_____

_____

# 92

Did you get into any trouble with
your friends? If yes, for what?

_____

_____

_____

_____

_____

_____

_____

_____

_____

_____

_____

_____

_____

# 93

Did your family practice a religion?
If so, describe the role religion played in your youth.

_____

_____

_____

_____

_____

_____

_____

_____

_____

_____

_____

_____

94

What was your neighborhood like?

_____

_____

_____

_____

_____

_____

_____

_____

_____

_____

_____

_____

_____

## 95

How independent were you as a kid?

_____

_____

_____

_____

_____

_____

_____

_____

_____

_____

_____

_____

# 96

What meals and foods remind you of your childhood?

_____

_____

_____

_____

_____

_____

_____

_____

_____

_____

_____

_____

# 97

What was a memorable "dad joke," "mom joke,"
or saying in your house?

_____

_____

_____

_____

_____

_____

_____

_____

_____

_____

_____

_____

# 98

Write down your grandparents' full names.
Describe your relationship with your grandparents.

_____

_____

_____

_____

_____

_____

_____

_____

_____

_____

_____

_____

_____

## 99

Was your dad's family a part of your life
growing up? If so, how often would you see them,
and what would you do together?

_____

_____

_____

_____

_____

_____

_____

_____

_____

_____

_____

_____

_____

# 100

Was your mom's family a part of your life growing up? If so, how often would you see them, and what would you do together?

_____

_____

_____

_____

_____

_____

_____

_____

_____

_____

_____

_____

_____

# 101

What was the biggest fight you got into as a kid?

_____

_____

_____

_____

_____

_____

_____

_____

_____

_____

_____

_____

# 102

What did you sometimes overhear
your parents fighting about?

_____

_____

_____

_____

_____

_____

_____

_____

_____

_____

_____

_____

# 103

What were your parents' political views?
How did that influence your views then and now?

_____

_____

_____

_____

_____

_____

_____

_____

_____

_____

_____

_____

# 104

If you were to describe anyone as your childhood rival
or nemesis, who would it be, and why?

_____

_____

_____

_____

_____

_____

_____

_____

_____

_____

_____

_____

# 105

What chores do you remember doing as a kid?

_____

_____

_____

_____

_____

_____

_____

_____

_____

_____

_____

_____

# 106

What kind of vacations did you take as a kid?

_____

_____

_____

_____

_____

_____

_____

_____

_____

_____

_____

_____

# 107

What songs do you most associate with childhood?

---

---

---

---

---

---

---

---

---

---

---

---

---

# 108

What do you remember about going through puberty?

_____

_____

_____

_____

_____

_____

_____

_____

_____

_____

_____

_____

_____

# 109

What did you want to be when you grew up?

_____

_____

_____

_____

_____

_____

_____

_____

_____

_____

_____

_____

# 110

Describe your first kiss.

_____

_____

_____

_____

_____

_____

_____

_____

_____

_____

_____

_____

_____

# ///

Who was your first boyfriend or girlfriend?
Describe him/her in detail.

_____

_____

_____

_____

_____

_____

_____

_____

_____

_____

_____

_____

_____

# 112

What story about your childhood does
your family refuse to stop telling?

_____

_____

_____

_____

_____

_____

_____

_____

_____

_____

_____

_____

# 113

What do you remember about junior high?

_____

_____

_____

_____

_____

_____

_____

_____

_____

_____

_____

_____

_____

# 114

What secrets did you keep as a kid/teenager?

_____

_____

_____

_____

_____

_____

_____

_____

_____

_____

_____

_____

_____

# 115

Who in your family helped guide you
in your teenage years?

_____

_____

_____

_____

_____

_____

_____

_____

_____

_____

_____

_____

# 116

What was your first experience dealing with death?

_____

_____

_____

_____

_____

_____

_____

_____

_____

_____

_____

_____

# 117

Were you closer to your mother or father
growing up? Did that change later on?

_____

_____

_____

_____

_____

_____

_____

_____

_____

_____

_____

_____

_____

_____

# 118

What outfit did you love as a teenager that
you wouldn't be caught dead in now?

_____

_____

_____

_____

_____

_____

_____

_____

_____

_____

_____

_____

_____

# 119

Whom did you idolize in high school?

_____

_____

_____

_____

_____

_____

_____

_____

_____

_____

_____

_____

What values did your parents instill in you?

_____

_____

_____

_____

_____

_____

_____

_____

_____

_____

_____

_____

_____

# 121

What was the first concert or show you attended?

_____

_____

_____

_____

_____

_____

_____

_____

_____

_____

_____

_____

_____

_____

# 122

What do you wish you had known in adolescence?

_____

_____

_____

_____

_____

_____

_____

_____

_____

_____

_____

_____

# 123

What skills did you develop or discover in adolescence?

_____

_____

_____

_____

_____

_____

_____

_____

_____

_____

_____

# 124

What was the meanest thing you remember
saying or doing in adolescence?

_____

_____

_____

_____

_____

_____

_____

_____

_____

_____

_____

_____

# 125

Who did you look out for when you were younger?

_____

_____

_____

_____

_____

_____

_____

_____

_____

_____

_____

_____

_____

# 126

Were you ever grounded? Why?

_____

_____

_____

_____

_____

_____

_____

_____

_____

_____

_____

_____

# 127

What was a Friday night like in high school?

_____

_____

_____

_____

_____

_____

_____

_____

_____

_____

_____

_____

_____

# 128

What did you and your parents fight about?

_____

_____

_____

_____

_____

_____

_____

_____

_____

_____

_____

_____

## 129

If you could go back and say something to
your teenage self, what would it be?

_____

_____

_____

_____

_____

_____

_____

_____

_____

_____

_____

_____

_____

# 130

What famous people did you look up to as a teenager?

_____

_____

_____

_____

_____

_____

_____

_____

_____

_____

_____

_____

# 131

Who was a bad influence on you as a teenager?

_____

_____

_____

_____

_____

_____

_____

_____

_____

_____

_____

# 132

In what ways was your home life
traditional or unconventional?

_____

_____

_____

_____

_____

_____

_____

_____

_____

_____

_____

_____

_____

# 133

Describe how involved you were
in sports then and now.

_____

_____

_____

_____

_____

_____

_____

_____

_____

_____

_____

_____

_____

# 134

What fears did you have as an adolescent?

_____

_____

_____

_____

_____

_____

_____

_____

_____

_____

_____

_____

_____

# 135

Describe your first teenage relationship.

_____

_____

_____

_____

_____

_____

_____

_____

_____

_____

_____

_____

_____

_____

# 136

What life change or curveball
did you experience growing up?

_____

_____

_____

_____

_____

_____

_____

_____

_____

_____

_____

_____

_____

_____

# 137

Was there a time in your teen years when
you felt invincible? Describe it.

_____

_____

_____

_____

_____

_____

_____

_____

_____

_____

_____

_____

_____

_____

# 138

What class do you remember most
from high school?

_____

_____

_____

_____

_____

_____

_____

_____

_____

_____

_____

_____

## 139

Who were you jealous of as a teenager?
Who might have been jealous of you?

_____

_____

_____

_____

_____

_____

_____

_____

_____

_____

_____

_____

_____

140

On a scale from hippie to helicopter, what
was the parenting like in your house?

_____

_____

_____

_____

_____

_____

_____

_____

_____

_____

_____

_____

# 141

What was the biggest lesson you learned
about friendship as a teenager?

_____

_____

_____

_____

_____

_____

_____

_____

_____

_____

_____

_____

_____

# 142

How did you envision your future
when you were a teenager?

---

---

---

---

---

---

---

---

---

---

---

# 143

What romantic or spontaneous moment stands out
when you think back on high school?

_____

_____

_____

_____

_____

_____

_____

_____

_____

_____

_____

_____

_____

# 144

How much partying did you do in high school?

_____

_____

_____

_____

_____

_____

_____

_____

_____

_____

_____

_____

_____

_____

# 145

Describe a time when someone
really had your back.

_____

_____

_____

_____

_____

_____

_____

_____

_____

_____

_____

_____

# 146

Describe how you learned to drive
and who taught you.

_____

_____

_____

_____

_____

_____

_____

_____

_____

_____

_____

_____

# 147

When did you get your driver's license,
and how did it feel?

_____

_____

_____

_____

_____

_____

_____

_____

_____

_____

_____

_____

# 148

When did you get your first car?
What make and color was it?
How did this make you feel?

_____

_____

_____

_____

_____

_____

_____

_____

_____

_____

_____

_____

# 149

What summer jobs did you have?

---------------------------------------

---------------------------------------

---------------------------------------

---------------------------------------

---------------------------------------

---------------------------------------

---------------------------------------

---------------------------------------

---------------------------------------

---------------------------------------

---------------------------------------

# 150

What adventures or travel experiences
did you have in your youth?

---------------------------------------

---------------------------------------

---------------------------------------

---------------------------------------

---------------------------------------

---------------------------------------

---------------------------------------

---------------------------------------

---------------------------------------

---------------------------------------

---------------------------------------

---------------------------------------

# 151

What kind of grades did you have in high school?
Were you and your parents happy with them?

_____

_____

_____

_____

_____

_____

_____

_____

_____

_____

_____

_____

_____

# 152

Describe your high school graduation day.

_____

_____

_____

_____

_____

_____

_____

_____

_____

_____

_____

_____

# 153

Who were your closest friends in high school?
How did these relationships shape you?

---

 

---

 

---

 

---

 

---

 

---

 

---

 

---

 

---

 

---

 

---

# 154

What exciting memories of high school do you have?

_____

_____

_____

_____

_____

_____

_____

_____

_____

_____

_____

_____

_____

# 155

What was your first experience with
alcohol or drugs, if any?

_____

_____

_____

_____

_____

_____

_____

_____

_____

_____

_____

_____

_____

# 156

What responsibilities did you have in high school?

_____

_____

_____

_____

_____

_____

_____

_____

_____

_____

_____

_____

# 157

If you went to the prom, whom did you go with,
and what do you remember most?

_____

_____

_____

_____

_____

_____

_____

_____

_____

_____

_____

_____

# 158

What kind of technology do you wish existed
(or didn't exist) when you were younger? Explain why.

_____

_____

_____

_____

_____

_____

_____

_____

_____

_____

_____

# 159

What was your first sexual experience like?

_____

_____

_____

_____

_____

_____

_____

_____

_____

_____

_____

_____

_____

160

Describe the day you got accepted into college
or the day you left for college.

_____

_____

_____

_____

_____

_____

_____

_____

_____

_____

_____

_____

_____

# 161

Who were your friends in college?
Are you still close with them?

_____

_____

_____

_____

_____

_____

_____

_____

_____

_____

_____

_____

162

What were your grades like in college?
How hard did you work?

_____

_____

_____

_____

_____

_____

_____

_____

_____

_____

_____

_____

_____

# 163

Are you happy with the college/path you chose after
high school, or would you do it differently?

_____

_____

_____

_____

_____

_____

_____

_____

_____

_____

_____

_____

164

What is your fondest memory of college?

_____

_____

_____

_____

_____

_____

_____

_____

_____

_____

_____

_____

_____

# 165

Which college professor had an
impact on you and why?

_____

_____

_____

_____

_____

_____

_____

_____

_____

_____

_____

_____

# 166

What is your least favorite memory of college?

_____

_____

_____

_____

_____

_____

_____

_____

_____

_____

_____

_____

# 167

What were your political views in college?
How do they differ, if at all, from your views today?

_____

_____

_____

_____

_____

_____

_____

_____

_____

_____

_____

_____

_____

_____

# 168

What did you learn about yourself in college?

_____

_____

_____

_____

_____

_____

_____

_____

_____

_____

_____

_____

## 169

Did your college experience prepare you for
the workforce? Why or why not?

_____

_____

_____

_____

_____

_____

_____

_____

_____

_____

_____

_____

# 170

What was your graduation like?
Describe how you felt, what you remember of the
ceremony, and who showed up to cheer you on.

_____

_____

_____

_____

_____

_____

_____

_____

_____

_____

_____

_____

/7/

What did you learn about your
parents as you got older?

_____

_____

_____

_____

_____

_____

_____

_____

_____

_____

_____

_____

# 172

If you could go back to one day from your youth,
which would it be, and why?

---
---
---
---
---
---
---
---
---
---
---
---

# 173

What were you naïve about as a young adult?

_____

_____

_____

_____

_____

_____

_____

_____

_____

_____

_____

_____

# 174

As a college graduate, what did you imagine
when you pictured your future?

_____

_____

_____

_____

_____

_____

_____

_____

_____

_____

_____

_____

## 175

What was your first "real" job,
and how good a fit was it?

_____

_____

_____

_____

_____

_____

_____

_____

_____

_____

_____

_____

_____

_____

# 176

Do you think you're a strong person?
List the reasons why or why not.

_____

_____

_____

_____

_____

_____

_____

_____

_____

_____

_____

_____

_____

# 177

List all of the things you like about yourself.

_____

_____

_____

_____

_____

_____

_____

_____

_____

_____

_____

_____

_____

# 178

What is your favorite word and why?

_____

_____

_____

_____

_____

_____

_____

_____

_____

_____

_____

_____

# 179

What do you think you were born to do?

_____

_____

_____

_____

_____

_____

_____

_____

_____

_____

_____

_____

_____

# 180

What is your favorite quote?

_____

_____

_____

_____

_____

_____

_____

_____

_____

_____

_____

_____

_____

# 181

What makes you cry like a baby?

_____

_____

_____

_____

_____

_____

_____

_____

_____

_____

_____

_____

# 182

What is the first thing you do in the morning?

_____

_____

_____

_____

_____

_____

_____

_____

_____

_____

_____

_____

_____

# 183

What is your bedtime routine,
and what does it say about you?

_____

_____

_____

_____

_____

_____

_____

_____

_____

_____

_____

_____

_____

# 184

Name the thing that annoys you the most,
and explain why it annoys you.

_____

_____

_____

_____

_____

_____

_____

_____

_____

_____

_____

_____

# 185

What secret have you kept until now?

_____

_____

_____

_____

_____

_____

_____

_____

_____

_____

_____

_____

# 186

What did you do on your twenty-first birthday?

_____

_____

_____

_____

_____

_____

_____

_____

_____

_____

_____

_____

# 187

What kind of people are you drawn to and why?

_____

_____

_____

_____

_____

_____

_____

_____

_____

_____

_____

_____

_____

# 188

What kind of people do you steer clear of and why?

_____

_____

_____

_____

_____

_____

_____

_____

_____

_____

_____

_____

# 189

Who or what makes you laugh?

_____

_____

_____

_____

_____

_____

_____

_____

_____

_____

_____

_____

_____

_____

190

What surprised you about becoming an adult?

_____

_____

_____

_____

_____

_____

_____

_____

_____

_____

_____

# 191

What makes you happy?

_____

_____

_____

_____

_____

_____

_____

_____

_____

_____

_____

_____

## 192

What makes you feel loved?

_____

_____

_____

_____

_____

_____

_____

_____

_____

_____

_____

# 193

What is the best thing that could
happen to you right now?

_____

_____

_____

_____

_____

_____

_____

_____

_____

_____

_____

_____

_____

# 194

What is the one thing you fear the most?

_____

_____

_____

_____

_____

_____

_____

_____

_____

_____

_____

_____

# 195

What are you proud of doing as an adult?

_____

_____

_____

_____

_____

_____

_____

_____

_____

_____

_____

_____

_____

# 196

Whom in your life do you treat the best?

_____

_____

_____

_____

_____

_____

_____

_____

_____

_____

_____

_____

# 197

Are you more of a talker or a listener?
Give an example.

_____

_____

_____

_____

_____

_____

_____

_____

_____

_____

_____

_____

_____

# 198

What advice would you give to your childhood self?

_____

_____

_____

_____

_____

_____

_____

_____

_____

_____

_____

_____

_____

# 199

What successes have you had in your life?

_____

_____

_____

_____

_____

_____

_____

_____

_____

_____

_____

_____

_____

200

What have you always believed in?

---------------------------------------

---------------------------------------

---------------------------------------

---------------------------------------

---------------------------------------

---------------------------------------

---------------------------------------

---------------------------------------

---------------------------------------

---------------------------------------

# 201

What failures have you experienced?
What did you learn from them?

_____

_____

_____

_____

_____

_____

_____

_____

_____

_____

_____

_____

# 202

Have you ever stolen anything?
If not, would you?

_____

_____

_____

_____

_____

_____

_____

_____

_____

_____

_____

_____

# 203

What emergencies have you witnessed or experienced?

_____

_____

_____

_____

_____

_____

_____

_____

_____

_____

_____

_____

_____

204

Have you ever been on television or wanted
to be? In what capacity?

_____

_____

_____

_____

_____

_____

_____

_____

_____

_____

_____

_____

_____

# 205

What is something that you've always loved doing?

---
---
---
---
---
---
---
---
---
---
---
---

# 206

If you could change one thing about your
life now, what would it be?

_____

_____

_____

_____

_____

_____

_____

_____

_____

_____

_____

# 207

To the best of your knowledge,
how do people perceive you?

_____

_____

_____

_____

_____

_____

_____

_____

_____

_____

_____

_____

## 208

How would you like others to perceive you?

_____

_____

_____

_____

_____

_____

_____

_____

_____

_____

_____

_____

209

Are you a procrastinator?
If not, what motivates you?

_____

_____

_____

_____

_____

_____

_____

_____

_____

_____

_____

_____

210

How much do you care about what
others think of you?

_____
_____
_____
_____
_____
_____
_____
_____
_____
_____
_____
_____

# 211

What does success mean to you?

_____

_____

_____

_____

_____

_____

_____

_____

_____

_____

_____

_____

_____

_____

# 212

Have you lived your life the way you wanted to?

---

---

---

---

---

---

---

---

---

---

---

---

---

# 213

What is your ideal day?

_____

_____

_____

_____

_____

_____

_____

_____

_____

_____

_____

_____

_____

# 214

Who is your ideal friend?
What characteristics would they have?

_____

_____

_____

_____

_____

_____

_____

_____

_____

_____

_____

_____

# 215

What was the first stamp on your passport, if any?

# 216

Where would you like to travel and why?

_____

_____

_____

_____

_____

_____

_____

_____

_____

_____

_____

_____

# 217

What do you wish you had done earlier?

_____

_____

_____

_____

_____

_____

_____

_____

_____

_____

_____

_____

_____

# 218

Which close relationships have stood the test
of time? Which ones have not?

_____

_____

_____

_____

_____

_____

_____

_____

_____

_____

_____

# 219

What is your favorite kind of music?

_____

_____

_____

_____

_____

_____

_____

_____

_____

_____

_____

_____

_____

# 220

What global or national issues
do you care about most?

_____

_____

_____

_____

_____

_____

_____

_____

_____

_____

_____

_____

_____

# 221

What experiences from your youth
still influence you today?

_____

_____

_____

_____

_____

_____

_____

_____

_____

_____

_____

_____

# 222

What are your thoughts and feelings about marriage?

_____

_____

_____

_____

_____

_____

_____

_____

_____

_____

_____

_____

_____

# 223

What family members were a constant support
to you after you left home?

_____

_____

_____

_____

_____

_____

_____

_____

_____

_____

_____

_____

# 224

What did you learn from your early
experiences with love?

_____

_____

_____

_____

_____

_____

_____

_____

_____

_____

_____

_____

# 225

Describe your first serious relationship.

_____

_____

_____

_____

_____

_____

_____

_____

_____

_____

_____

_____

_____

# 226

What is the longest relationship you've ever had?
Why do you think it lasted that long?

_____

_____

_____

_____

_____

_____

_____

_____

_____

_____

_____

_____

# 227

What is the closest you have come
to finding your soulmate?

_____

_____

_____

_____

_____

_____

_____

_____

_____

_____

_____

_____

# 228

Describe your wedding or the best
party you've ever thrown.

_____

_____

_____

_____

_____

_____

_____

_____

_____

_____

_____

_____

_____

# 229

How do you feel about having kids?

_____

_____

_____

_____

_____

_____

_____

_____

_____

_____

_____

_____

_____

# 230

How do you feel about kids in general?

_____

_____

_____

_____

_____

_____

_____

_____

_____

_____

_____

_____

# 231

How do you feel about divorce?

_____

_____

_____

_____

_____

_____

_____

_____

_____

_____

_____

_____

# 232

What is the funniest story your friends
could tell about you?

_____

_____

_____

_____

_____

_____

_____

_____

_____

_____

_____

_____

# 233

What is the best memory you have
of your grandparents?

_____

_____

_____

_____

_____

_____

_____

_____

_____

_____

_____

_____

_____

# 234

How do you stay healthy?

_____

_____

_____

_____

_____

_____

_____

_____

_____

_____

_____

_____

# 235

What was the highlight of your life so far?

_____

_____

_____

_____

_____

_____

_____

_____

_____

_____

_____

_____

_____

# 236

What is the most spontaneous thing
you have done as an adult?

_____

_____

_____

_____

_____

_____

_____

_____

_____

_____

_____

# 237

When have you been heartbroken?

_____

_____

_____

_____

_____

_____

_____

_____

_____

_____

_____

# 238

Describe your children or the children in your life
and what you've learned from them.

_____

_____

_____

_____

_____

_____

_____

_____

_____

_____

_____

# 239

Describe yourself as a parent or how you
imagine you would be as a parent.

_____

_____

_____

_____

_____

_____

_____

_____

_____

_____

_____

_____

240

What makes a great parent?

_____

_____

_____

_____

_____

_____

_____

_____

_____

_____

_____

_____

# 241

What are you proud to have taught
the children in your life?

_____

_____

_____

_____

_____

_____

_____

_____

_____

_____

_____

# 242

What do you wish your parents had done
differently, if anything?

_____

_____

_____

_____

_____

_____

_____

_____

_____

_____

_____

_____

# 243

What are your hopes and dreams for your kids
or for the kids in your life?

_____

_____

_____

_____

_____

_____

_____

_____

_____

_____

_____

_____

_____

# 244

What is the most beautiful thing you've ever seen?

_____

_____

_____

_____

_____

_____

_____

_____

_____

_____

_____

_____

# 245

What is the scariest thing you've seen or experienced?

_____

_____

_____

_____

_____

_____

_____

_____

_____

_____

_____

# 246

What do you do when you need to be inspired?

_____

_____

_____

_____

_____

_____

_____

_____

_____

_____

_____

_____

# 247

What makes a perfect husband/wife/partner?

_____

_____

_____

_____

_____

_____

_____

_____

_____

_____

_____

_____

_____

# 248

Describe your best friend.

_____

_____

_____

_____

_____

_____

_____

_____

_____

_____

_____

_____

# 249

What kind of a friend are you?

_____

_____

_____

_____

_____

_____

_____

_____

_____

_____

_____

_____

_____

# 250

How close are you to your parents?
What role do they play in your life?

_____

_____

_____

_____

_____

_____

_____

_____

_____

_____

_____

_____

# 251

What are you still trying to prove to your parents?

_____

_____

_____

_____

_____

_____

_____

_____

_____

_____

_____

_____

_____

# 252

What have you already proven to your parents?

_____

_____

_____

_____

_____

_____

_____

_____

_____

_____

_____

# 253

What mistakes have you made in
friendships or relationships?

_____

_____

_____

_____

_____

_____

_____

_____

_____

_____

_____

_____

# 254

Whom do you miss the most?

_____

_____

_____

_____

_____

_____

_____

_____

_____

_____

_____

# 255

What new interests have you developed as an adult?

_____

_____

_____

_____

_____

_____

_____

_____

_____

_____

_____

# 256

What is your favorite meal to make or eat?
Describe a memory related to this meal.

_____

_____

_____

_____

_____

_____

_____

_____

_____

_____

_____

# 257

What role do you play in your family now?

_____

_____

_____

_____

_____

_____

_____

_____

_____

_____

_____

_____

_____

_____

# 258

Whom can you count on no matter what?

_____

_____

_____

_____

_____

_____

_____

_____

_____

_____

_____

_____

# 259

What was one of the most defining
moments in your life?

_____

_____

_____

_____

_____

_____

_____

_____

_____

_____

_____

_____

# 260

What do you want people to say about you one day?

_____

_____

_____

_____

_____

_____

_____

_____

_____

_____

_____

_____

# 261

Describe the person who teaches you the most.

---

 

---

 

---

 

---

 

---

 

---

 

---

 

---

 

---

 

---

 

---

 

---

# 262

Which play, song, or movie has had a strong impact
on your life? Describe the impact it had.

_____

_____

_____

_____

_____

_____

_____

_____

_____

_____

_____

_____

_____

# 263

What life lesson were you quick to learn?

_____

_____

_____

_____

_____

_____

_____

_____

_____

_____

_____

_____

# 264

What life lesson did you learn the hard way?

_____

_____

_____

_____

_____

_____

_____

_____

_____

_____

_____

_____

_____

# 265

What can you teach others?

_____

_____

_____

_____

_____

_____

_____

_____

_____

_____

_____

# 266

Describe something you want to learn more about.

_____

_____

_____

_____

_____

_____

_____

_____

_____

_____

_____

_____

# 267

Describe the jobs that suited you best.
What does this say about you?

_____

_____

_____

_____

_____

_____

_____

_____

_____

_____

_____

_____

_____

# 268

What job do you hope to have someday?

_____

_____

_____

_____

_____

_____

_____

_____

_____

_____

_____

_____

# 269

Describe your philosophy of life.

_____

_____

_____

_____

_____

_____

_____

_____

_____

_____

_____

_____

_____

## 270

Who is your professional role model and why?

_____

_____

_____

_____

_____

_____

_____

_____

_____

_____

_____

_____

_____

# 271

Describe a struggle you've had at your job
and how you got through it.

_____

_____

_____

_____

_____

_____

_____

_____

_____

_____

_____

_____

_____

# 272

What's the biggest mistake you've
made in your life or career?

_____

_____

_____

_____

_____

_____

_____

_____

_____

_____

_____

_____

## 273

What is the best thing you did for your career?

_____

_____

_____

_____

_____

_____

_____

_____

_____

_____

_____

_____

_____

# 274

How do you balance work, play, and family time?

_____

_____

_____

_____

_____

_____

_____

_____

_____

_____

_____

_____

_____

## 275

If you could give any advice to younger people starting a career, what would you tell them?

_____

_____

_____

_____

_____

_____

_____

_____

_____

_____

_____

_____

# 276

What is something you hope to accomplish one day?

_____

_____

_____

_____

_____

_____

_____

_____

_____

_____

_____

# 277

How do you feel about your country?

_____

_____

_____

_____

_____

_____

_____

_____

_____

_____

_____

# 278

If you had to live in a different country,
where would you live, and why?

_____

_____

_____

_____

_____

_____

_____

_____

_____

_____

_____

_____

# 279

What gives you strength?

_____

_____

_____

_____

_____

_____

_____

_____

_____

_____

_____

_____

280

When have you risen to the occasion?

_____

_____

_____

_____

_____

_____

_____

_____

_____

_____

_____

# 281

What (or who) gives you the creeps?

_____

_____

_____

_____

_____

_____

_____

_____

_____

_____

_____

_____

## 282

When have you turned lemons into lemonade?

_____

_____

_____

_____

_____

_____

_____

_____

_____

_____

# 283

What are your biggest vices?

_____

_____

_____

_____

_____

_____

_____

_____

_____

_____

_____

_____

# 284

Describe how you feel about your appearance.
How is this different than in the past?

_____

_____

_____

_____

_____

_____

_____

_____

_____

_____

_____

_____

# 285

About what do you have doubts?

_____

_____

_____

_____

_____

_____

_____

_____

_____

_____

_____

_____

_____

# 286

Describe how your fashion tastes have
changed over the years.

_____

_____

_____

_____

_____

_____

_____

_____

_____

_____

_____

_____

# 287

Describe your financial status
and how you feel about it.

_____

_____

_____

_____

_____

_____

_____

_____

_____

_____

_____

_____

_____

## 288

How important is it to you to make more money?
What would you do with it?

_____

_____

_____

_____

_____

_____

_____

_____

_____

_____

_____

_____

_____

# 289

What role does art play in your life?

_____

_____

_____

_____

_____

_____

_____

_____

_____

_____

_____

_____

_____

290

What age have you enjoyed the most so far?

_____

_____

_____

_____

_____

_____

_____

_____

_____

_____

_____

# 291

List all of the best places you have visited in your life.

_____

_____

_____

_____

_____

_____

_____

_____

_____

_____

_____

_____

292

Describe your favorite place in the world.

_____

_____

_____

_____

_____

_____

_____

_____

_____

_____

_____

_____

# 293

Describe what you do when you're upset.

_____

_____

_____

_____

_____

_____

_____

_____

_____

_____

_____

# 294

What are some habits you've developed as an adult?

_____

_____

_____

_____

_____

_____

_____

_____

_____

_____

_____

_____

# 295

Where do you get your news?

_____

_____

_____

_____

_____

_____

_____

_____

_____

_____

_____

_____

_____

# 296

What historic events have happened
during your lifetime?

---

 

---

 

---

 

---

 

---

 

---

 

---

 

---

 

---

 

---

 

---

 

---

# 297

What causes are near and dear to your heart?

_____

_____

_____

_____

_____

_____

_____

_____

_____

_____

_____

_____

# 298

What law deserves to be broken?

_____

_____

_____

_____

_____

_____

_____

_____

_____

_____

_____

_____

## 299

What rule do you always follow?

_____

_____

_____

_____

_____

_____

_____

_____

_____

_____

_____

# 300

Whom do you still admire after
all these years and why?

_____

_____

_____

_____

_____

_____

_____

_____

_____

_____

_____

_____

_____

# 301

Who do you consider a part of your inner circle?

_____

_____

_____

_____

_____

_____

_____

_____

_____

_____

_____

_____

# 302

Describe a relationship that greatly
improved as you got older.

_____

_____

_____

_____

_____

_____

_____

_____

_____

_____

_____

_____

_____

# 303

What are the qualities you believe
all functional families have in common?

_____

_____

_____

_____

_____

_____

_____

_____

_____

_____

_____

304

Which relationships in your life are really
healthy? Really unhealthy?

_____

_____

_____

_____

_____

_____

_____

_____

_____

_____

_____

## 305

What would you change about your family dynamic if you could?

_____

_____

_____

_____

_____

_____

_____

_____

_____

_____

_____

_____

# 306

Whose death affected you the most?

_____

_____

_____

_____

_____

_____

_____

_____

_____

_____

_____

_____

## 307

What occurs to you as you reflect back on your life?

_____

_____

_____

_____

_____

_____

_____

_____

_____

_____

_____

# 308

What are you most grateful for in life?

_____

_____

_____

_____

_____

_____

_____

_____

_____

_____

_____

_____

# 309

What do you value most and why?

_____

_____

_____

_____

_____

_____

_____

_____

_____

_____

_____

_____

## 310

When do you feel like your life truly began?

_____

_____

_____

_____

_____

_____

_____

_____

_____

_____

_____

_____

_____

# 311

What advice moved you and continues to guide you?

_____

_____

_____

_____

_____

_____

_____

_____

_____

_____

_____

_____

# 312

What more do you want out of life?

_____

_____

_____

_____

_____

_____

_____

_____

_____

_____

_____

# 313

What is the strangest thing you've ever experienced?

_____

_____

_____

_____

_____

_____

_____

_____

_____

_____

_____

# 314

What goals and dreams have you worked toward?

---

---

---

---

---

---

---

---

---

---

---

---

# 315

What do you know about your ancestors?
What do you want to know?

_____

_____

_____

_____

_____

_____

_____

_____

_____

_____

_____

_____

# 316

What do you think has stayed the same about you
all your life? What has changed?

_____

_____

_____

_____

_____

_____

_____

_____

_____

_____

_____

_____

_____

# 3/7

What's the one thing you've always
wanted but still don't have?

---
---
---
---
---
---
---
---
---
---

# 318

What's the most memorable phone call
you've ever received or made?

_____

_____

_____

_____

_____

_____

_____

_____

_____

_____

_____

_____

# 319

What is your typical day like now? What part
of your routine would you like to change, if any?

_____

_____

_____

_____

_____

_____

_____

_____

_____

_____

_____

_____

_____

# 320

What do you do for fun?

_____

_____

_____

_____

_____

_____

_____

_____

_____

_____

_____

# 321

What age do you feel right now and why?

_____

_____

_____

_____

_____

_____

_____

_____

_____

_____

_____

# 322

What should everyone do in their twenties?

_____

_____

_____

_____

_____

_____

_____

_____

_____

_____

_____

_____

# 323

What should everyone do in their thirties?

_____

_____

_____

_____

_____

_____

_____

_____

_____

_____

_____

_____

# 324

What should everyone do in their forties?
Fifties? Sixties? Beyond?

_____

_____

_____

_____

_____

_____

_____

_____

_____

_____

_____

# 325

In which decade do you think you
hit your peak? Explain.

_____

_____

_____

_____

_____

_____

_____

_____

_____

_____

_____

_____

# 326

Which birthday were you less than
eager to experience? Why?

_____

_____

_____

_____

_____

_____

_____

_____

_____

_____

_____

_____

# 327

What's the hardest thing about growing older?
What's the best thing?

_____

_____

_____

_____

_____

_____

_____

_____

_____

_____

_____

_____

# 328

What do you think it means
to grow old gracefully?

_____

_____

_____

_____

_____

_____

_____

_____

_____

_____

_____

_____

# 329

What role does/should technology play in our lives?

_____

_____

_____

_____

_____

_____

_____

_____

_____

_____

_____

_____

What do you want to do with the
next ten years of your life?

_____

_____

_____

_____

_____

_____

_____

_____

_____

_____

_____

_____

_____

## 331

How does retirement sound to you?

---

---

---

---

---

---

---

---

---

---

---

# 332

Describe a person or situation from your childhood
that had a profound effect on you.

_____

_____

_____

_____

_____

_____

_____

_____

_____

_____

_____

_____

# 333

Describe your guilty pleasures.

_____

_____

_____

_____

_____

_____

_____

_____

_____

_____

_____

_____

# 334

What kind of books do you enjoy reading?

_____

_____

_____

_____

_____

_____

_____

_____

_____

_____

_____

# 335

What have you thrown away in your life
that you wish you held on to?

---

---

---

---

---

---

---

---

---

---

---

# 336

What material item have you held on to
that's important to you and why?

_____

_____

_____

_____

_____

_____

_____

_____

_____

_____

_____

# 337

How do you define a "good life"
or a "successful life"?

_____

_____

_____

_____

_____

_____

_____

_____

_____

_____

_____

_____

# 338

What do you see as your place or purpose in life?
How did you come to that conclusion?

_____

_____

_____

_____

_____

_____

_____

_____

_____

_____

_____

_____

_____

# 339

What makes you unique?

_____

_____

_____

_____

_____

_____

_____

_____

_____

_____

_____

_____

# 340

If you could go back and relive any part
of your life, what it would be?

_____

_____

_____

_____

_____

_____

_____

_____

_____

_____

_____

_____

## 341

In times of stress, what got you through?

_____

_____

_____

_____

_____

_____

_____

_____

_____

_____

_____

_____

# 342

What fears have you overcome with age?

_____

_____

_____

_____

_____

_____

_____

_____

_____

_____

_____

_____

# 343

When have you relied on your instincts?

_____

_____

_____

_____

_____

_____

_____

_____

_____

_____

_____

_____

# 344

What are you still learning about yourself?

_____

_____

_____

_____

_____

_____

_____

_____

_____

_____

_____

# 345

What have you accepted about yourself?

---

 

---

 

---

 

---

 

---

 

---

 

---

 

---

 

---

 

---

 

---

# 346

How great a role does faith play in your life now?

_____

_____

_____

_____

_____

_____

_____

_____

_____

_____

_____

# 347

What is your favorite day of the week and why?

_____

_____

_____

_____

_____

_____

_____

_____

_____

_____

_____

# 348

What family story should live on forever?

_____

_____

_____

_____

_____

_____

_____

_____

_____

_____

_____

_____

# 349

What is the best way to grow old?

_____

_____

_____

_____

_____

_____

_____

_____

_____

_____

_____

_____

_____

# 350

What makes you feel younger than you are?

_____

_____

_____

_____

_____

_____

_____

_____

_____

_____

_____

_____

# 351

Describe your feelings about the next generation.

_____

_____

_____

_____

_____

_____

_____

_____

_____

_____

_____

_____

# 352

Who is the love of your life?

_____

_____

_____

_____

_____

_____

_____

_____

_____

_____

_____

_____

# 353

What question have you always
wanted to ask someone?

_____

_____

_____

_____

_____

_____

_____

_____

_____

_____

_____

_____

# 354

What famous person would you like to
meet in real life if you could?

_____

_____

_____

_____

_____

_____

_____

_____

_____

_____

_____

_____

# 355

Do you have any regrets involving your
parents, siblings, or loved ones?

_____

_____

_____

_____

_____

_____

_____

_____

_____

_____

_____

_____

_____

# 356

What was the most difficult year of your life and why?

_____

_____

_____

_____

_____

_____

_____

_____

_____

_____

_____

_____

# 357

What was the best year of your life and why?

_____

_____

_____

_____

_____

_____

_____

_____

_____

_____

_____

_____

# 358

About what have you completely
changed your mind?

_____

_____

_____

_____

_____

_____

_____

_____

_____

_____

_____

_____

# 359

What could you do when you were younger
that you miss being able to do now?

_____

_____

_____

_____

_____

_____

_____

_____

_____

_____

_____

_____

_____

# 360

What can you do now that you weren't able
to do when you were younger?

_____

_____

_____

_____

_____

_____

_____

_____

_____

_____

_____

_____

# 361

What do you want to focus on achieving next?

_____

_____

_____

_____

_____

_____

_____

_____

_____

_____

_____

_____

_____

# 362

What were some of the major themes
in your life so far?

_____

_____

_____

_____

_____

_____

_____

_____

_____

_____

_____

_____

# 363

Do you think there is life after death? Explain.

_____

_____

_____

_____

_____

_____

_____

_____

_____

_____

_____

_____

_____

# 364

What mark would you like to leave on the world?

_____

_____

_____

_____

_____

_____

_____

_____

_____

_____

_____

# 365

What do you want people to say about you someday?

_____

_____

_____

_____

_____

_____

_____

_____

_____

_____

_____

_____

_____